peeler

baking cup

strainer

garlic press

½ teaspoon

1/2

1 cup

scissors

spatula

baking cup

mixing spoon

look and cook
SNACKS

a first
book of
recipes
in
pictures

valorie fisher

ASTRA YOUNG READERS

AN IMPRINT OF ASTRA BOOKS FOR YOUNG READERS
New York

Look and Cook was created with young chefs in mind, those who might not yet be confident readers but are adventurous eaters and enthusiastic helpers in the kitchen. Through simple pictures, these visual recipes allow kids to understand and follow each step that goes into preparing a given food. This unique cookbook format encourages independence and means kids can take the lead in the kitchen, asking for assistance as they need it. Of course, we do recommend adults support kid chefs as they follow these recipes, especially in gathering ingredients and equipment beforehand and giving help whenever they see 🖐.

Kids will enjoy the process, the math, the mess, the magic, the cleanup (maybe), and, of course, sharing what they've created!

 2 Servings or amount the recipe makes

 **10 minutes** Time needed for the recipe or a step

 Step supervised or done by a grown-up

clock

saucepan

stovetop

blender

sink

oven

apron

1 cup

½ cup

⅓ cup

¼ cup

large bowl

small bowl

mixing spoon

sharp knife

pastry brush

ice-cream scoop

can opener

grater

toothpick

nonstick, oven-safe
parchment paper

parchment paper

garlic press

blunt scissors

kitchen towel

melon baller

funnel

baking cup

microwave

freezer

refrigerator

stool

tablespoon

teaspoon

½ teaspoon

1/4 teaspoon

blunt knife

juicer

1 cup liquid measure

pint jar

fork

ice pop mold

small bowl

cutting boards

spoon

8"x 8" baking pan

oven mitt

strainer

muffin tin

baking sheet

tall glass

small glass

Read the recipe

Wash your hands

Wash all fruits and vegetables

Ask for help anytime you need it

Gather your kitchen tools

Gather your ingredients

FLOUR

Hazelnut Spread

BAKING POWDER

parchment paper

Have fun

Help clean up

MILK

Mixing ingredients

Measuring butter

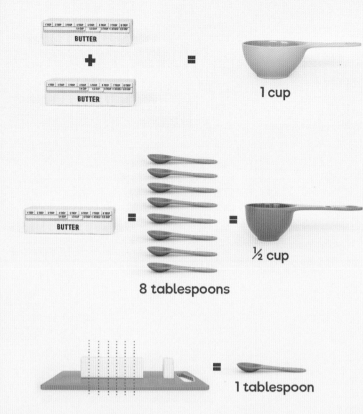

BUTTER + BUTTER = 1 cup

BUTTER = 8 tablespoons = ½ cup

= 1 tablespoon

Juicing

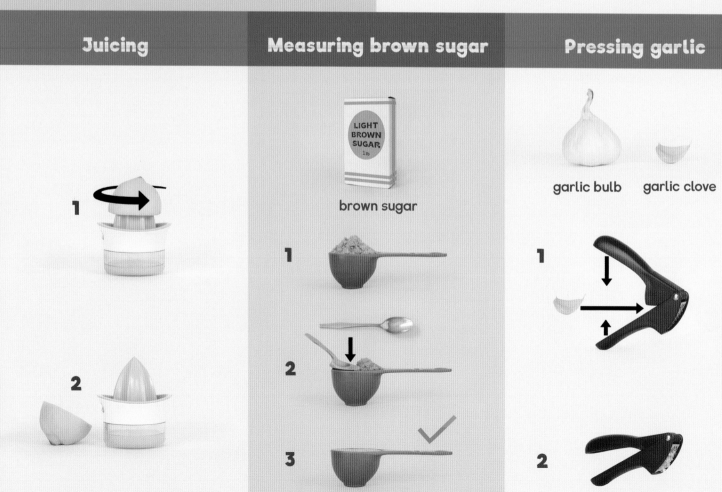

Measuring brown sugar

LIGHT BROWN SUGAR 1 lb

brown sugar

Pressing garlic

garlic bulb   garlic clove

Measuring cups & spoons

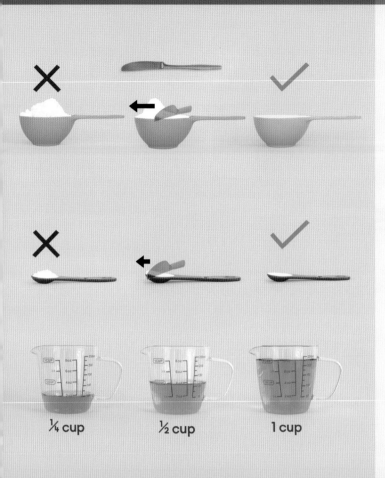

¼ cup   ½ cup   1 cup

Cracking an egg

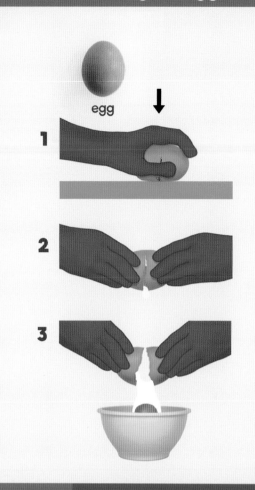

egg

1
2
3

Pinch of salt

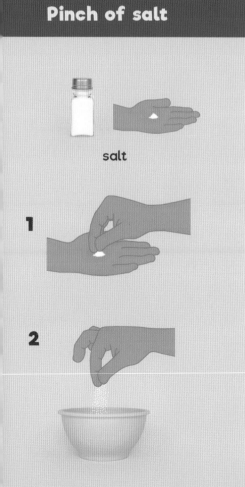

salt

1
2

Snipping herbs

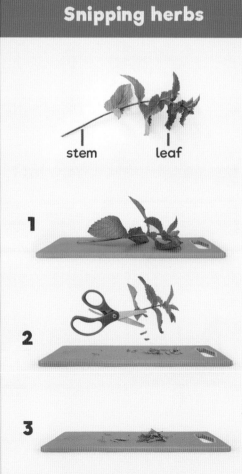

stem   leaf

1
2
3

Baking toothpick test

1   toothpick

crumbs

2   +2 minutes

clean

3

MEASURING, MIXING, AND MORE

7

FROOTHIE

  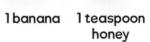

½ cup milk	1 banana	1 teaspoon honey	½ cup frozen mango	1 cup strawberries

1 teaspoon		blunt knife	
	½ cup		
1 cup liquid measure	1 cup	small cutting board	blender

1

2

3

4

5

6

LIME FIZZ

1 lime

1 tablespoon honey

1 cup seltzer

1 tablespoon

spoon

sharp knife

1 cup liquid measure

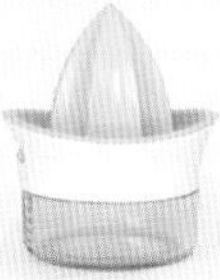

small cutting board

juicer

tall glass

1 ✋

2

3

4

5

6

9

BANUTTER

peanut butter

1 banana

slice of bread

small cutting board

blunt knife

1

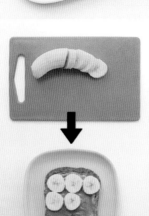

2

3

4

PICKLED PEANUT

 peanut butter

 * bread and butter pickles

 slice of bread

 make your own **EASY·PEASY PICKLES** 28

 blunt knife

fork

1

2

3

4

AVOCADO SMASHUP

1 ripe avocado

1 tablespoon lime juice

1 teaspoon olive oil

pinch of salt

1 teaspoon

1 tablespoon

juicer

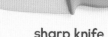

fork

spoon

sharp knife

small bowl

small cutting board

 ✗    ✗    ✗    ✓    ✗

1

2

3

4

5

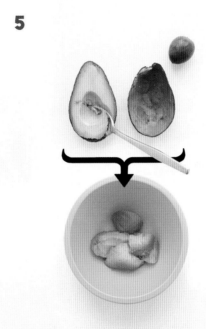

6

7

8

1

2

3

13

QUESA RICA DILLA

1 flour tortilla

⅓ cup Mexican-style shredded cheese

½ teaspoon olive oil

⅓ cup

½ teaspoon

parchment paper

pastry brush

oven mitt

small baking sheet

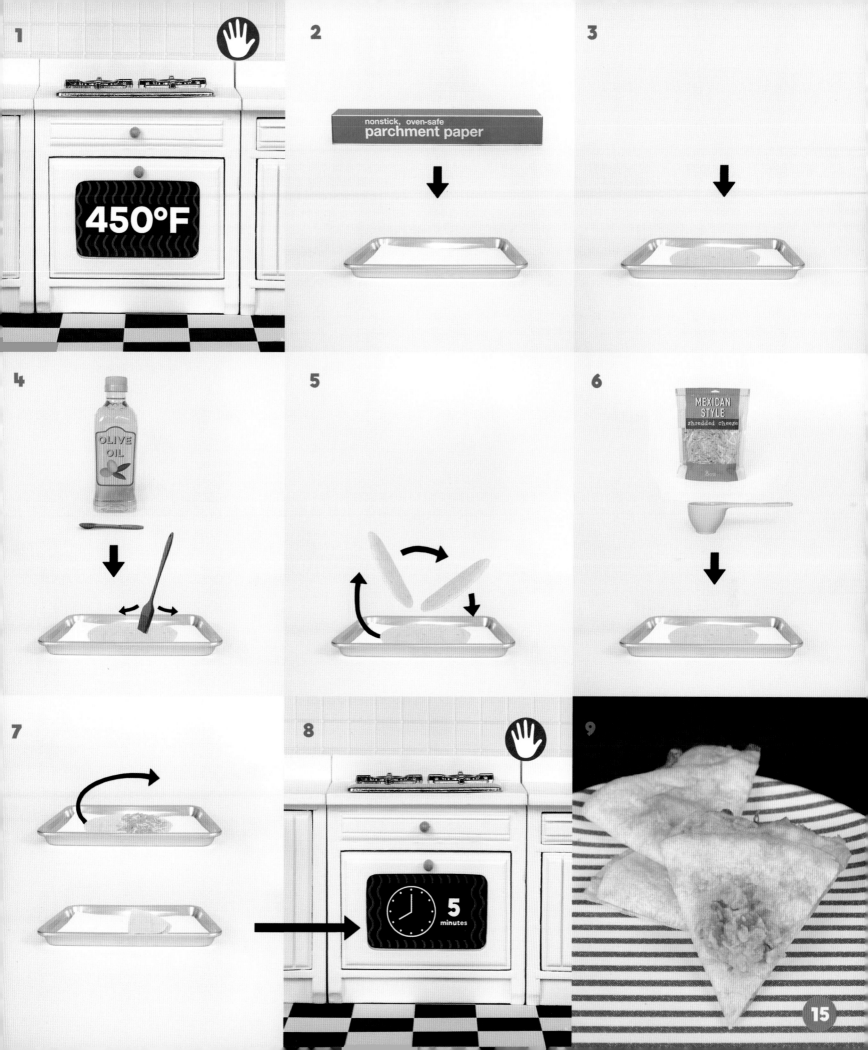

1 450°F

2 nonstick, oven-safe parchment paper

3

4 OLIVE OIL

5

6 MEXICAN STYLE shredded cheese

7

8 5 minutes

9

15

MOZZAMATO SALAD

1 cup
cherry tomatoes
halved

⅓ cup
mini mozzarella
balls

1 basil leaf

1 teaspoon
olive oil

pinch of salt

⅓ cup

1 cup

1 teaspoon

blunt scissors

spoon

sharp knife

small bowl

small cutting board

1

2

3

4

5

6

YUMMUS

 4

 **15 minutes**

1 can chickpeas

3 tablespoons lemon juice

3 tablespoons tahini

½ teaspoon salt

1 clove garlic

½ teaspoon

spoon

1 tablespoon

sharp knife

small cutting board

can opener

garlic press

juicer

blender

strainer

small bowl

1

2

3

Chickpeas

15 oz

4

5

6

Tahini
ground
sesame
seeds

+
+

+
+

7

8

9

19

NAANIZZA

🍴 1

🕐 **15** minutes

1 mini naan bread

1 tablespoon pasta sauce

¼ cup shredded mozzarella

½ teaspoon olive oil

1 basil leaf

½ teaspoon

1 tablespoon

blunt scissors

parchment paper

oven mitt

¼ cup

pastry brush

small baking sheet

1 400°F

2 nonstick, oven-safe parchment paper

3

4 OLIVE OIL

5 TOMATO SAUCE 16oz

6 MOZZARELLA shredded cheese 8oz

7

8 10 minutes

9

21

PINK POLKA·DOT SALAD

 1

 **10** minutes

1 cup watermelon balls

½ teaspoon lime juice

4 mint leaves

2 tablespoons crumbled feta

1 teaspoon olive oil

½ teaspoon

1 tablespoon

1 cup

1 teaspoon

melon baller

juicer

spoon

sharp knife

blunt scissors

small bowl

large cutting board

1

2

3

4

5

6

FETA

OLIVE OIL

7

8

9

CUCUMBER COOL

4

15 minutes

1 cucumber

1 clove garlic

1 tablespoon lemon juice

1 cup plain Greek yogurt

¼ teaspoon salt

1 sprig of dill

1 cup

sharp knife

¼ teaspoon

juicer

garlic press

1 tablespoon

spoon

grater

blunt scissors

kitchen towel

small bowl

small bowl

small cutting board

WRAP & ROLL

 8

 **30** minutes

1 tube crescent rolls

yellow mustard

4 ham slices

8 tablespoons
shredded cheddar cheese

baking sheet

large cutting board

1 tablespoon

blunt knife

parchment paper

oven mitt

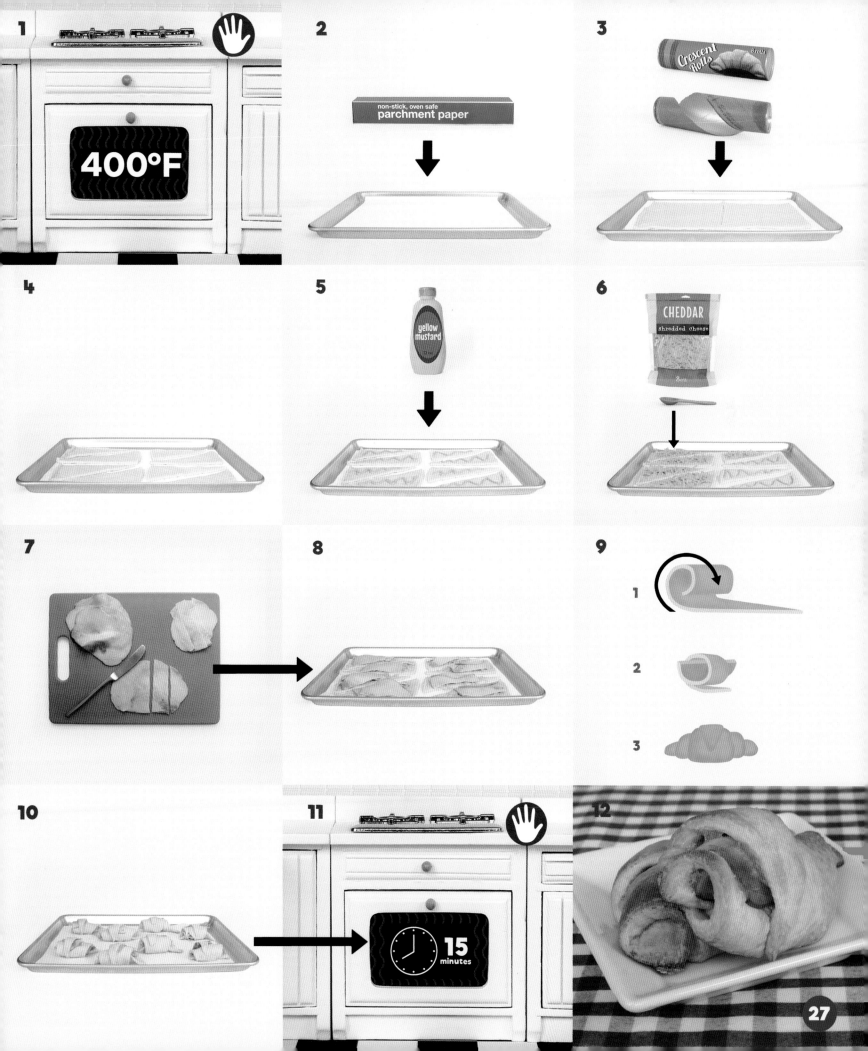

1

400°F

2

non-stick, oven safe
parchment paper

3

Crescent Rolls

4

5

yellow mustard

6

CHEDDAR
shredded cheese

7

8

9

1

2

3

10

11

15 minutes

12

Crescent Rolls

27

EASY·PEASY PICKLES

 **2 pints**

 **25 + 2**
minutes   days

5 mini cucumbers

1 small onion

1 cup
apple cider vinegar

¾ cup sugar

1 tablespoon
sea salt

¼ cup water

½ teaspoon
turmeric

1 teaspoon
celery seed

1 teaspoon
mustard seed

2 pint jars

saucepan

1 cup
liquid measure

½ teaspoon

sharp knife

1 teaspoon

1 tablespoon

¼ cup

spoon

funnel

large cutting board

 **EASY·PEASY PICKLES** will keep for
2 months in the refrigerator!

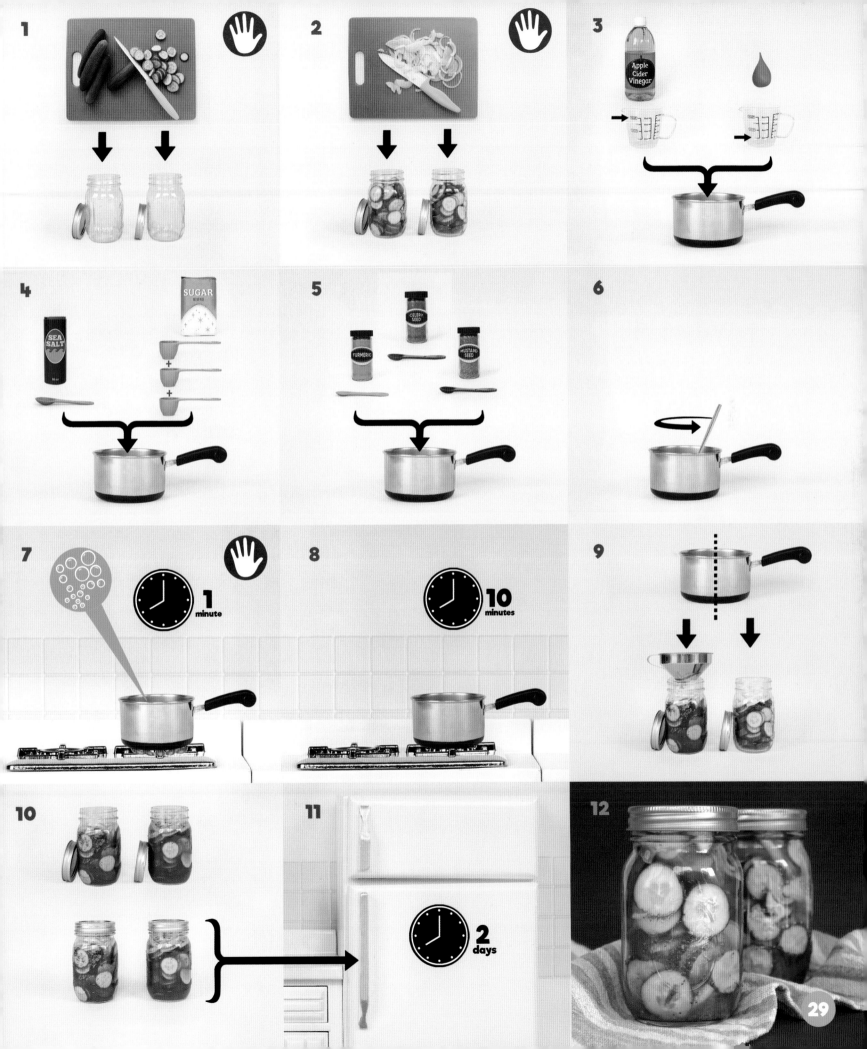

29

NUTTER NUGGET

½ cup
peanut butter

¾ cup
rolled oats

¼ cup
unsweetened
coconut flake

2 tablespoons
mini chocolate chips

2 tablespoons
maple syrup

2 tablespoons
dried cranberries

2 tablespoons
chia seeds

1 tablespoon

mixing spoon

¼ cup

½ cup

large bowl

31

BERRIES & CLOUDS

 1

 **10** minutes

¼ cup
blueberries

¼ cup
raspberries

1 teaspoon
maple syrup

½ cup
plain yogurt

1 tablespoon
sliced almonds

1 teaspoon

1 tablespoon

¼ cup

½ cup

small glass

spoon

small bowl

BANUFFIN

 **12**    **30 minutes**

1½ cup flour

1 cup light brown sugar

3 very ripe bananas

1 egg

⅓ cup canola oil

1 teaspoon baking soda

1 teaspoon vanilla

½ teaspoon salt

½ teaspoon

1 teaspoon

1 cup liquid measure

spoon

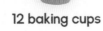
12 baking cups

fork

mixing spoon

toothpick

1 cup

½ cup

muffin tin

large bowl

oven mitt

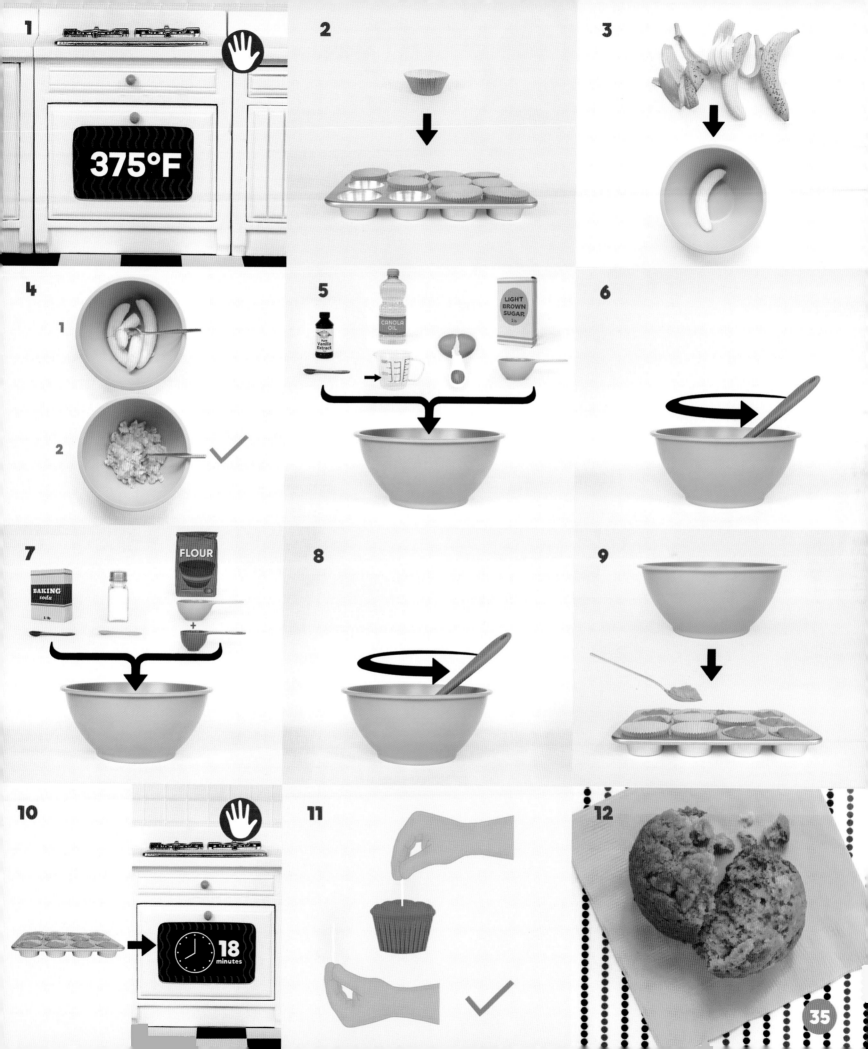

CHOCO CHEW

 24

 **20** minutes

1 cup flour

1 cup hazelnut spread

½ cup chocolate chips

2 teaspoons baking powder

1 egg

¼ teaspoon salt

½ cup

1 cup

oven mitt

¼ teaspoon

1 teaspoon

mixing spoon

nonstick, oven-safe
parchment paper

parchment paper

large bowl

2 baking sheets

1 350°F

2 nonstick, oven-safe **parchment paper**

3 FLOUR | BAKING POWDER +

4 Semi-Sweet Chocolate Chips | Hazelnut Spread

5

6 1"

7

8 9 minutes

9

37

SQUARE CHERRY

 16   🕐 1 hour

2 cups
flour

1½ cup
rolled oats

⅔ cup
light brown sugar

1 cup
cherry jam

½ teaspoon salt

1 cup
soft butter

⅓ cup
sliced almonds

parchment paper

⅓ cup

½ teaspoon

blunt knife

½ cup

spoon

8" x 8" baking pan

1 cup

small cutting board

large bowl

oven mitt

FROSTY FRUIT

🍽 6   🕐 **15** minutes **+** **6** hours

3 cups
seedless watermelon

1 cup
blueberries

2 tablespoons
lime juice

1 tablespoon
honey

1 tablespoon
sharp knife

1 cup

juicer

ice-cream scoop

ice pop mold

large cutting board

blender

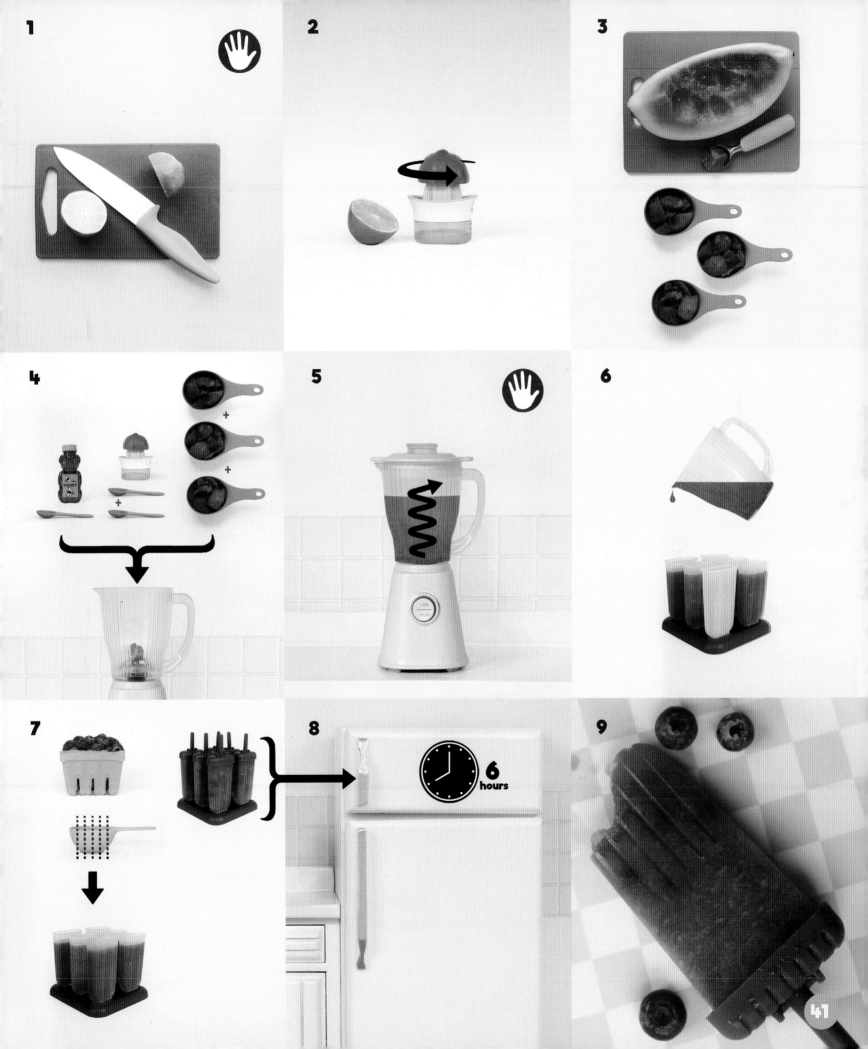

41

Missing an ingredient? Substitute!

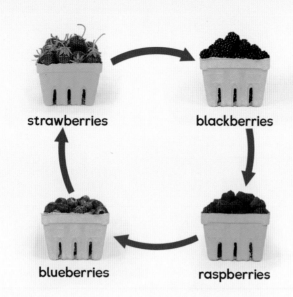

strawberries → blackberries → raspberries → blueberries → strawberries

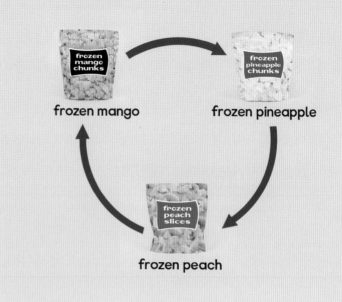

frozen mango → frozen pineapple → frozen peach → frozen mango

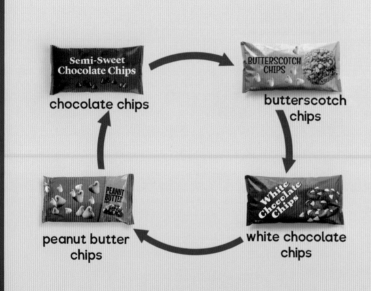

chocolate chips → butterscotch chips → white chocolate chips → peanut butter chips → chocolate chips

watermelon → cantaloupe → honeydew → watermelon

Mix it up! Add extra ingredients!

BANUFFIN

+

1 cup

chocolate chips

OR

raisins

OR

chopped walnuts

honey

maple syrup

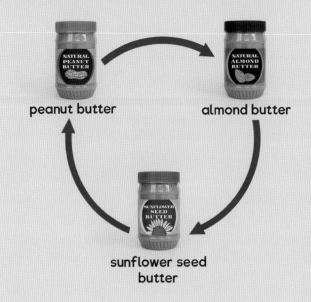

peanut butter

almond butter

sunflower seed
butter

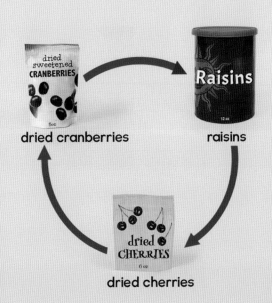

dried cranberries

raisins

dried
CHERRIES

dried cherries

sliced almonds

chopped walnuts

chopped pecans

NAANIZZA

3 slices pepperoni

1 tablespoon   sliced olives

Friends that cook together, stay together.
For cooking companions Karen, Jacquie,
Lovey & Lee —VF

Astra Young Readers
An imprint of Astra Books for Young Readers,
a division of Astra Publishing House
astrapublishinghouse.com
Printed in China

ISBN: 978-1-6626-2044-7 (hc)
ISBN: 978-1-6626-2045-4 (eBook)
Library of Congress Control Number: 2022921738

First edition

10 9 8 7 6 5 4 3 2 1

Design by Valorie Fisher and Barbara Grzeslo
The text is set in Riffic Medium.
The titles are set in Riffic Bold.

Acknowledgments:
I am enormously grateful to Karen Hatt
for her insight and keen eye. I would like
to thank Susan Saccardi and Susie Ott
for sharing their culinary wisdom;
Jacque Schiller and Gina Maolucci for
their endless enthusiasm; Olive Cowan,
Laura Lopez, and Sebastian Pia for their
word jumbling skills; and David Cowan
for his unflappable support. Last but not
least, a huge thanks to my terrific team
of recipe testers: Hazel, Theodora, Nat,
Cam, Oliver, and Ellis.

About the art in this book:
A photographer, set designer, and
adventurous home cook, Valorie Fisher
combined all of these skillsets to create
the photo illustrations in this book. Valorie
constructs miniature sets incorporating
kitchen tools, dollhouse miniatures, fruits,
vegetables, and other ingredients, and
then takes a picture.

can opener

½ cup

juicer

mixing spoon

grater

bowl

peeler

spatula